SONGS

Hello there. Thank you for choosing us.

Enjoy the music by hitting the notes.

Surprise Everyone

ALPHA

ART

Starboy

The Weeknd

Sweater Weather

The Neighbourhood

3

Someone You Love by Lewis Capaldi

4

Make You Mine - PUBLIC

Circles

Post Malone

8

The Chainsmokers & Coldplay - Something Just Like This

Life Goes On - BTS

SHAUN feat. Conor Maynard - Way Back Home

Passenger - Let Her Go

16

Watermelon Sugar

Harry Styles

18

Path Of The Wind Ost My Neighbor Totoro

Avicii - Waiting For Love

Wiz Khalifa - See You Again ft. Charlie Puth

TONES AND I - DANCE MONKEY

Someone You Loved

Lewis Capaldi

We Wish You A Merry Christmas

I am Not The Only One by Sam Smith

How Far I'll Go Ost Moana

Time To Say Goodbye - Andrea Bocelli & Sarah Brightman

JINGLE BELLS

K-391 & Alan Walker - Ignite

Coldplay - Hymn For The Weekend

Shallow Ost A Star Is Born

Pretty Savage - BLACKPINK

Shania Twain - You're Still The One

I Want To Break Free By Queen

Hosanna - Hillsong Worship

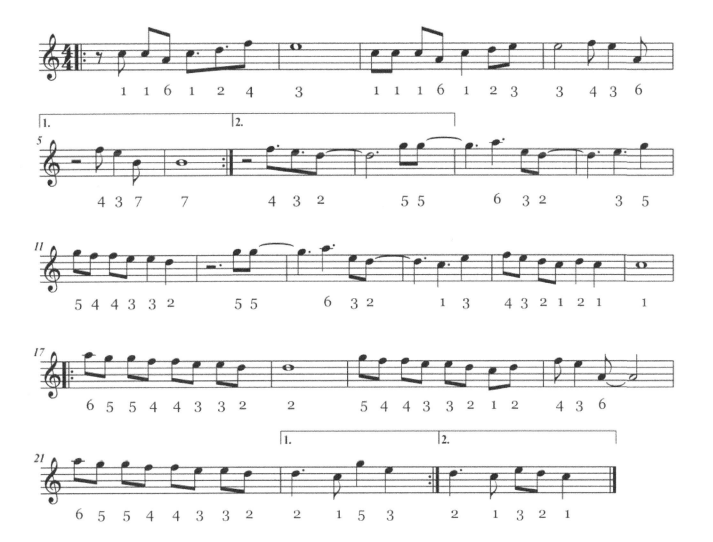

SAD by XXXTentacion

A Whole New World Ost Aladdin

Shout To The Lord - Hillsong Worship

Rewrite The Stars Ost The Greatest Showman

ROCKABYE - Clean Bandit feat. Sean Paul & Anne-Marie

Naomi Scott - Speechless

ON (BTS)

Josh Groban - You Raise Me Up

Bryan Adams - Heaven

Tick Tock - Clean bandit and Mabel feat. 24kGoldn

Stay

The Kid LAROI, Justin Bieber

47

2

5' 5' 5' 6' 5' 4'   6 6 6 6 4 4 4   4 5 5   6 6 6 4 4 4   4 5 5   4 5 4

6 6 6 4 4 4   4 5 5   4 6 6 6 4 4 4   4 5 5   4 5 4   3' 3' 4'   5 5 4

5 5 4 5 6   5 5 4 5 5 5 4   5 6 3 4   4 6 5   4 6 5

4 6 5   4 6 5   2'   4 4 4   4 5 4   3' 2' 1'

48

Sad Song by We The Kings ft Elena Coats

Joy To The World

The Scientist By Coldplay

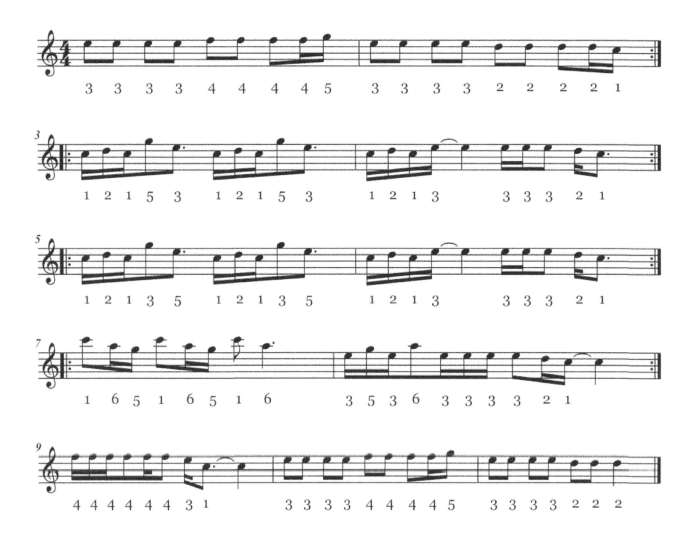

Take Me to Church

Hozier

♩ = 67

HAVANA By Camila Cabello

7 Rings

Ariana Grande

55

All Of Me

John Legend

56

Another Love

Tom Odell

Cheap Thrills

Sia

Faded

Alan Walker

Lean On

Major Lazer

Levitating

Dua Lipa

♩ = 115

3' 5' 3' 5'   2' 4' 6 6   3' 5' 3' 5'   2' 4' 6 6   3' 3'3' 3' 2' 2'2' 2' 1'1' 1'1' 7 7 7 7

6

6 6 6 6 6 5 6   6   3' 3' 3' 3' 2' 2' 2' 2' 1' 1' 1' 1' 7 7 7 7   6 6 6 6 6 5 6

9

6 6 6 6 7   1'1'1'1'2'   3' 3' 3' 3' 5' 3'   3' 3' 3' 3' 2'2' 2'2' 1'1' 1'1' 7 7 7 7   6 6 6 6 6 5 6

13

3' 2' 1'   3' 2'1'6 5   3' 2' 1'   3' 2'1'6 5   3' 2' 1'   3' 2'1'6 5   6 6' 5' 4' 3'   1' 1'

17

3'   2' 2'   2' 2'   2' 2' 1' 1'   3'   2' 2'   2' 2' 2' 1' 6   3' 2' 1' 6 5

21

3'   2' 2'   2' 2'   2' 2' 1' 1'   3'   2' 2'   2' 2' 2' 1' 6   3' 2' 1' 6 5

61

Thank you very much for choosing me. I hope you enjoyed. waiting for your positive feedback

★★★★★

Made in the USA
Las Vegas, NV
16 December 2024

14342415R00037